S0-BLH-896

THE BOOK OF BEER

THE BOOK OF

BEER

Randy Burgess

Ariel Books

Andrews and McMeel
Kansas City

Photographs on pp. 2, 6, 27, 32–33, 36, 47, 49,
59, 73, and endsheets © 1997 by Bill Yenne

Illustrations courtesy of Anchor Brewing
Company; British Tourist Authority; Hop
Growers of America; Merchant du Vin
Corporation; North Dakota Barley Council; Sierra
Nevada Brewing Company; and UPI/Corbis-
Bettmann

ISBN: 0-8362-2639-9
Library of Congress Catalog Card Number:
96-85941

CONTENTS

INTRODUCTION

The next time you drink a beer, whether it be ale or lager, supermarket suds or exotic import, take a moment before you quaff; take a moment and contemplate. Let the bubbles drift upward through their liquid medium, which can be almost any color from black to palest yellow: brown as mahogany, tawny as teak, or ruddy as an English pub keeper's winking face. What a curious thing is beer, what an odd combination of history, personal memory, banality, and bliss!

It is probably the oldest alcoholic beverage in the world, having been discovered and cultivated by the Sumerians, those diligent and inventive predecessors of the Babylonians, at least eight thousand years ago and conceivably much earlier than that. It also has a strong spiritual history: The Egyptians believed it nourished them not only in life but in the afterlife, and during the Middle Ages in Europe, the master brewers were Trappist monks.

Beer has also been, throughout history, the drink of the common man and

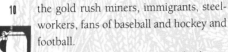

10

woman—the English farmer and his wife, the gold rush miners, immigrants, steel-workers, fans of baseball and hockey and football.

In all likelihood, it is your drink too. You may hoist it only occasionally, to cool a fiery Chinese dish or to warm an evening in a strange hotel. Or you may regard it as one of the necessary pleasures of life, no more to be abandoned than conversation, laughter, and fellowship.

What you may not know, however, is the fastidious rituals, the thousand secrets, the myriad identities of beer. Why did it flourish almost entirely in the countries of Europe? What is the difference between lager and ale, porter and stout, a pilsner and a pint of bitter? Is it okay to buy beer that hasn't been refrigerated? Is it okay to *drink* beer that hasn't been refrigerated? What does it mean to say that a beer is hoppy? And, for that matter, what are hops?

Relax. Take a sip. Leaf through these pages and learn. You've got plenty of time; after all, a truth common to beer everywhere is that it is never drunk in a hurry. That may be the best secret of all.

EARLY BEER

Get Thee to a Monastery

After the collapse of the Roman Empire, with feudalism and Christianity spreading across the face of Western Europe, monasteries became the centers of learning, the preservers of civilized culture and thought. One of the things they preserved was beer. In fact, beer experts tell us, monks were the first truly scientific brewers, improving the technology involved so that beer tasted better and kept longer.

Monks in Bohemia and Germany, for example, were the first to discover that adding the bitter flower of the hop plant both prevented spoiling and nicely balanced the sweetness of malted barley. Today, virtually all beer uses hops as a basic ingredient. Bavarian monks also invented lager—beer fermented and matured at colder temperatures (originally in Alpine caves) to give it a cleaner, smoother taste. Lager became increasingly popular in the centuries to come, and today, what most of us in the United States mean by beer is actually lager.

Why did monks, whom we think of as living strict lives of prayer, scholarship, and hard labor, brew beer in the first place? For one thing, like so many others in medieval Europe, monks liked beer because it was safe to drink. Plain water could carry disease, but beer never did, because it was boiled during the process of

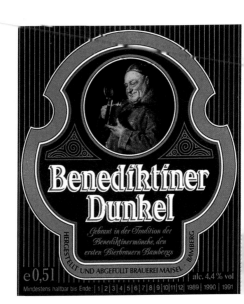

brewing. For another, the rules of monastic life demanded that abbeys and monasteries be self-sufficient, so that the brothers could completely isolate themselves from the sinful (and dangerous) outside world. This meant that each had to have its own garden, water supply, and so on—including its own brewery. Later, monks also brewed beer to serve to pilgrims.

A half-dozen Trappist abbeys, all but one of them in Belgium, still brew beer today. These are generally powerful, fruity ales.

English Ale

Around the twelfth century, brewing beer at home became commonplace in England. The preferred variety was not the monks' lager, but good old English ale: beer (according to a now-archaic definition) made without hops.

Taverns and alehouses sprang up rapidly, and their products were sometimes vile; in London, the government appointed ale-connors to inspect for quality. One way the ale-connor did this was to spill a little on a bench, sit on it for a while, and then see if his breeches had stuck to it. If they had, it meant that the ale hadn't fermented long enough and still contained too much undigested sugar. The brewer was promptly fined.

BEER ACROSS THE WATER

The Pilgrims might have left England far behind, but not their English thirst. In sober fact, when they arrived on these shores in 1620, having endured a long Atlantic crossing, the English emigrants hoped to continue southward before landing to find a gentler climate. They changed their minds and made do with Plymouth only because (as one diarist wrote) "our victuals [were] much spent, especially our Beere."

Rich colonists at Jamestown, Virginia, were able to afford barley for their beer, but poorer ones fueled their fermentation with such substitutes as Indian corn, potatoes, or even Jerusalem artichokes. Puritans relied on similar measures, as a popular New England song pointed out:

BEER ACROSS THE WATER

If barley be wanting to make into malt,
We must be content and think it no fault,
For we can make liquor to sweeten our lips
Of pumpkins, and parsnips, and walnut tree
chips.

In 1635, only a few years after the colonization of Manhattan, Dutch settlers built the first brewery on the island. As the colonies in general grew and thrived, so did taverns, breweries, and brewhouses, so that travelers and towndwellers alike could enjoy ale and beer aplenty.

Brewing was a fairly common activity

in the New World; among our founding fathers, Samuel Adams, James Madison, Thomas Jefferson, and George Washington all brewed beer on at least an amateur basis, and often with keen interest. Jefferson in particular kept detailed notes of his brewing techniques. He preferred his methods to those of public brewers, who in his opinion tried to make too much beer from too little grain—with the result that their product was "meagre and often vapid." Let it also be noted that the protesters who staged the Boston Tea Party in 1773 fueled themselves beforehand on rum and strong ale, drunk at the Green Dragon Tavern.

We Switch to Lager

According to one estimate, by the early 1800s more than one hundred breweries in the United States were producing nearly three hundred thousand barrels a year. The nation still was growing, and the production of beer would grow with it.

German immigrants to Philadelphia set up breweries to make the lager that already dominated in Europe. In the first half of the nineteenth century, Americans drank mostly ales, porters, and stouts (see definitions below in the section "What's in a Wort?"); by the late 1800s, almost everyone was drinking lager. Smooth, light lagers seemed easier to drink in warm American weather than the strong, sweet ales and porters that had been perfected in England and Ireland. And with its clarity of complexion, lager was ideally suited for display in the transparent beer glasses coming into style. Then disaster struck for beer.

Prohibition: Bad Times and Worse Home Brew

On January 16, 1920, the Volstead Act took effect, and Prohibition plunged hundreds of thousands of beer drinkers, not to mention drinkers of harder stuff, into dryness and gloom. (Andrew Volstead, by the way, was the Minnesota congressman who sponsored the law. Few remember him today.) People being what they are, they didn't stop drinking, nor did they entirely rely on bootleggers to keep them supplied. Some started making the stuff themselves.

Malt (partially sprouted barley) was still legally available for baking—and malt is one of the primary ingredients for making beer. To this, homebrewers would add a slug of sugar and a cake of Fleishmann's yeast. Unfortunately, the ingredients were crude, the technique cruder, and many amateur brewers lacked the patience to wait for their seething, bubbling masses to settle down and stabilize. The result would usually be strong. It would also be as clear as mud and possess all the character and maturity of liquid bread dough. As William Mares puts it in *Making Beer,* "Beer drinkers came out of Prohibition with both an enormous thirst and a violent distaste for home brew." This torture ended in 1932, when Prohibition was repealed.

Beer in Our Time: From Suds to Microbreweries

In the decades that followed Prohibition, regional beer styles prospered: At one point there were more than seven hundred breweries in the United States. Unfortunately, this happy state of affairs was destined to end.

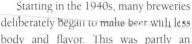

Starting in the 1940s, many breweries deliberately began to make beer with less body and flavor. This was partly an attempt to appeal to women, and partly a way of allowing the brewers to make use of corn and rice—inexpensive grains, but less assertive than barley and wheat. The resulting (bland) product could be marketed anywhere to anybody.

Such homogeneity found favor with the new supermarket chains that had begun to replace local grocers across the country. Moreover, big brewers could afford national advertising, whereas regional breweries could not. In addition, Americans in the years after World War II became increasingly mobile, weakening their regional loyalties. By the mid-1970s, fewer than seventy breweries survived, and it seemed as if Americans would be forever doomed to suds. But hope was unexpectedly at hand.

That same decade of big-brewery acquisition, the 1970s, also saw the first burst of microbreweries. The movement began in Britain and became immediately and amazingly popular. In 1975, the concept crossed the Atlantic to America, where the first microbrewery opened in Sonoma, California. That brewery, New Albion, did not survive—but it inspired countless others, which today carry on a young but proud tradition.

Ales, stouts, porters, wheat beers, fruit beers, winter ales—all these and more can be had from American microbreweries, although you may have to sniff around to find stores willing to stock the more esoteric varieties. Brewpubs (restaurants that make their own unpasteurized beer on the premises) have also become widely popular, as has the frustrating but ultimately rewarding craft of homebrewing. Michael Jackson, a noted British beer authority, puts it this way: "The world always knew that beer was a noble and complex drink, but, for a moment in history, that was forgotten. Now it is being remembered."

What's in a Wort?
A Quick Lesson in
Beer Basics

In order to be a true beer connoisseur, you should be able to call a beer "hoppy" and know what it is you're saying, or nod wisely when the subject of malting is brought up at your local pub.

Even if you're not interested in hoasting and have little or no desire to ever do any malting yourself, you'll find you enjoy your beer more when you understand exactly what it is you are drinking, how it was made, and how it differs from other beers. At the very least, you'll gain the confidence to try beers you've never tried before—stouts as dark as baker's chocolate, or aromatic ales, or that strange arrival from Belgium with the stranger label and even stranger ingredients.

XXXX

Some basic brewing terms:

➶ **Malt**. In the beginning was malt, and it was good. Specifically, malt is grain (most often barley, but also wheat, oats, or rye) that has been soaked in water just long enough to sprout, and then dried. Malting develops enzymes; enzymes, during the brewing process, help convert the starch in the grain into sugars; and sugars give yeast something to feed on. Malting isn't as simple as it sounds, because everything from the variety of barley to how it is dried will affect a beer's taste. For example, malt for porters and

stouts is not only dried but roasted, just as coffee beans are roasted.

➙ **Grist.** Grist is malt and other grains that have been milled, or ground, so that they can be used to make a mash (see below under "Wort"). As one writer plaintively notes, the old figure of speech should be "grist from the mill," not "grist for the mill."

⇥ **Yeast.** Like wine, the first beers were fermented by wild yeasts, borne by breezes through the air. (Some beers in Belgium, called lambics, are still made this way.) These tiny one-celled fungi digest sugars, producing carbon dioxide and alcohol. Most breweries nowadays rely on strains that have been refined over the centuries to produce flavors that are always special and in some cases unique. Since the process of fermentation is invisible, it was once believed by European

Lindemans Frick is one of the
five best beers in the world.
It is produced at Lindemans
farm brewery and wheat.
base of barley and wheat.
After wild fermentation the
beer is aged in oak barrels. Fresh
cherries are added creating a
secondary fermentation.
Serve cold.

0 85725 10812 5

brewers to be a gift from God.

╍╍◦ **Hops.** The hop vine produces a
bitter, fragrant blossom. It was apparently
first added to beer in the Middle Ages by
a Benedictine abbess named Hildegarde
to balance the sweet malt and act as a

CONTENTS: 750 ML (25.4 FL OZ)

SPONTANE GISTING · FERMENTATION SPONTANEE

Merchant DuVin COMPILATION

KRIEK

LAMBIC

BELGIAN CHERRY FLAVORED ALE

BREWED WITH NATURAL INGREDIENTS

Water, Barley-Malt, Wheat, Hops, Yeast, and Fresh Cherries

PRODUCT OF BELGIUM

BROUWERIJ LINDEMANS

VLEZENBEEK, BELGIUM

Sole U.S. Agents Merchant DuVin Corp. Seattle, WA 98121

preservative. Before that, beer was flavored not by hops but by such herbs and
spices as rosemary, juniper, sweet willow,
and yarrow. Nowadays, if you love the
taste of hops, you are deemed a sophisti-
cated beer connoisseur, but if you shun it,

you are considered hopelessly naive.

➤ **Wort.** Pronounced wert. In brewing, water is filtered through a bed of grist, or ground-up malted grain. This process is called mashing. The resulting runoff, saturated with sugars and other natural chemicals released by the malt, is the wort. The wort is boiled; hops are added, and later, yeast; finally it is set aside to ferment.

➣ **Tun.** A huge kettle, whether enclosed or open, in which beer is mashed, fermented, aged, and otherwise persuaded to become tasty.

⇒ **Bottom-fermenting.** Yeast that does its business at the bottom of the tun rather than the top, and in chilly conditions rather than warm; the result is lagered beer, clear to the eye and smooth to the tongue. (For contrast, see "Ale" below.)

⇒ *Reinheitsgebot.* A historic law enacted in 1516 by the Duke of Bavaria, which decreed that beer could only be made from malt, hops, and water. Anything else was considered an impurity. German brewers still follow this law today—in marked contrast to the big

American names, which for decades have used corn and rice as inexpensive additions.

Now that you can speak like a brewmaster, let's define just a few of the classic styles of beer:

→ **Abbey beer.** Ale made by secular brewers in Belgium, and modeled on the beers produced by Trappist monks—that is, fruity and strong.

→ **Ale.** Beer brewed by yeast that ferments at the top of the kettle, making a foamy head that is later skimmed off. Ales

are fermented at a relatively warm temperature, about that found in a moderately cool cellar, and should be drunk at about that temperature for maximum enjoyment. They tend to have a more complex character than lagers.

~⊨ **Beer.** Just to make it clear: Beer is the embracing term for beverages fermented from grains and seasoned with hops. It includes both lager and ale, even though Americans often think it means only the former and Britons, the latter.

~⊨ **Berliner Weisse.** Any of the "white beers" made in Berlin from malted wheat and barley. As fruity and acidic as good champagne and, with its low alcohol content and light body, an excellent summer drink. Similar wheat or white (take your pick) beers are made elsewhere in Germany, as well as in Belgium;

the Belgians do not malt the wheat, and they sometimes add such spices as orange peel and coriander.

⇒ **Bitter.** A dry English ale, often served on draft in the pubs. When Morse, the brilliant but erratic detective of Colin Dexter's murder mysteries, asks the man behind the bar for "a pint of your best bitter," this is what he wants.

⇝ **Bock.** A popular dark lager in Germany and the United States. For a lager, bock is surprisingly full-bodied, strong, and sweet. It is what the casual beer drinker often means by "dark beer."

⇝ **India pale ale.** A fruity, hoppy ale, and not so much pale in the glass as blushing or bronze. Pale ale has been made in Britain for more than a century. The India style was developed for ship-

CA REDEMPTION VALUE

Purest Ingredients

Finest Quality

SIERRA NEVADA®

PALE ALE

NET CONTENTS 12 FL. OZ.

© 1989 S.N.BR. CO.

BREWED & BOTTLED BY SIERRA NEVADA BREWING CO., CHICO, CA

ment to that country in the 1800s when it was still a British colony; the high hop content was intended to guard against spoilage during the long sea voyage.

Excellent India pale ales are now made by
microbreweries in the Seattle area.

➥ **Lager.** A bottom-fermented beer,

THE BOOK OF BEER

typically matured for months in cold conditions. An example of a classic lager is pilsner, which displays not only fragrance and softness but a hoppy aftertaste.

Mild. What the British drink in pubs when they're not drinking bitter. Tastes like its name.

➼ **Porter.** Nearly black in appearance because the malt used to make it is first roasted in a kiln. The roasted flavor nicely contrasts with the fruitiness typical of an ale—but don't go calling porter an ale, or you'll have some irritated Brits after you. Very similar to stout.

⇥ **Steam beer.** A hybrid that uses lager yeast, but is fermented at the warm temperatures usually reserved for ales. The style originated in California in the days before mechanical refrigeration; now it is used by only a few breweries,

57

BREWED AND BOTTLED BY ANCHOR BREWING CO., SAN FRANCISCO, CA FROM ALL BARLEY MALT · CONTENTS 12 FLUID OZ.

ANCHOR STEAM BEER

Made in San Francisco since 1896

most notably San Francisco's Anchor.

Stout. Like porter, but only more so. The classic example of stout is a Guinness.

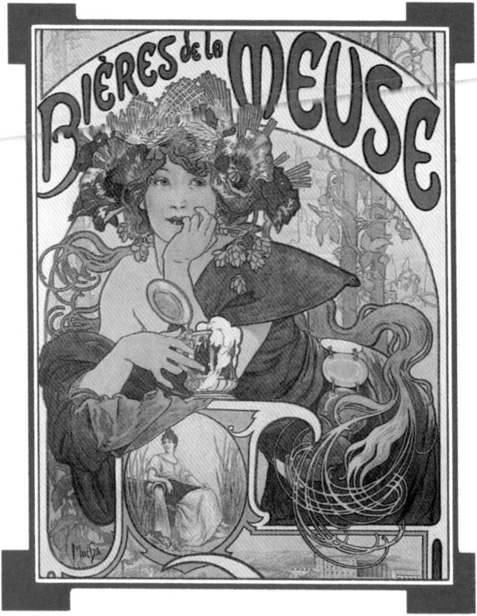
BIÈRES de la MEUSE
Mucha

TRIVIA, TALK, AND TALES ABOUT BEER

*B*eer, especially the dark, full-bodied kind, has historically been regarded—and quite rightly—as not only drink, but also food, and even medicine.

Our Neolithic ancestors gathered and steeped grains of wild barley to produce the first primitive beers. This brewing process decreased the stomach-irritating properties of barley, as well as increasing the B vitamins and essential amino acids (although they didn't know this).

In England during the Renaissance, ale was commonly drunk by itself as supper. Often it was thickened with butter, sugar, and beaten eggs, and in Scotland it was thickened with oatmeal.

The English also thought highly of beer's

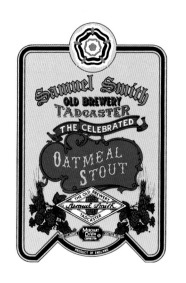

medicinal value. Ales flavored with herbs were called physical ales. In the spring, ale was mixed with scurvy grass to provide much-needed vitamin C after the long winter.

In Germany, doctors from time immemorial have prescribed beer for its nutritious and relaxing qualities to nursing mothers, insomniacs, and the over-tense.

Hammurabi, the Babylonian ruler, incorporated a number of edicts concerning beer into his famous code of laws, inscribed on a column at Susa, a ruined

city in Iran. Owners of beer parlors who
overcharged customers were drowned to
death. Those found to have diluted their
beer were imprisoned within their own
vats. High priestesses caught loitering in
such establishments were burnt to death.
These injunctions might best be described
as consumer protection with a vengeance.

In medieval England, a bride traditionally
served ale to the guests at her marriage
feast. This was called *bryd ealo*, or bride
ale; the words evolved over the centuries
to become our modern-day *bridal*.

Beer can accompany more than hot dogs, hamburgers, ribs, and Chinese or Mexican cuisine, says Michael Jackson, the foremost British champion of beer. A hoppy pilsner sharpens the flavor of cod and other whitefish; a bock can balance a rich ragout; fruity Trappist ales are a stunning backdrop to fresh asparagus; and dry stout, Jackson relates with obvious pleasure, "seems to tickle the salty flavor of oysters."

A 1988 survey ranked West Germany as the top beer-drinking nation, followed by East Germany (this was of course prior to Germany's reunification), Czechoslovakia,

and Denmark. The United States ranked twelfth in consumption, but first in production.

Stark nought, looking white and thick as [if] pigs had wrestled in it, smoky and ropy.

—A description of sixteenth-century Cornish ale, from Andrew Boorde's *A Compendyous Regyment, or A Dyetary of Helth*

Cheap beer is the only means to keep rum out!

> —General James Edward Oglethorpe,
> founder of the American colony
> of Georgia

BE GOOD OR BEGONE

NOTICE, NO BACK ROOM IN HERE
FOR LADIES

> —Signs in McSorley's Old Ale House,
> opened in 1854 on Seventh Street,
> New York City

That which gladdens your heart
Brings joy to our heart as well.
Our liver is well-satisfied, our heart is
    happy.
You have poured your blessing on the
    promising stone;
You have inspired a time of cooperation
    and prosperity.

May you dwell closely with the
  goddess Ninkasi!
She will offer to pour your beer and
  wine;
Let her guidance bring you joyfulness in
  all things

— From a five-thousand-year-old toast
    to a woman tavern keeper
    in Mesopotamia

Saloon life radiated a bleary, beery charm. . . . A saloon gave a man a chance to air his political opinions; it gave him masculine privacy, a feeling of belonging, easy credit (despite the curt notices on the wall to the contrary), escape from nagging household problems, and what's more, a free lunch.

—Michael and Ariane Batterberry
On the Town in New York

Are we to believe that the foundations of western civilization were laid by an ill-fed people living in a perpetual state of partial intoxication?

—Botanist Paul Manglesdorf, arguing against the theory that agriculture arose because of beer

"Do you ever drink wine?" people ask me, as though beer were a prison rather than a playground.

—British beer expert Michael Jackson

*But the wonderful thing about porter
was the way it made you stand aside, or
rather float aloft like a cherub rolling on
a cloud, and watch yourself with your
legs crossed, leaning against a bar
counter, not worrying about trifles but
thinking deep, serious, grown-up
thoughts about life and death.*

—Frank O'Connor
"The Drunkard"

*When I got home the Amstel beer was
still there in the refrigerator, a gift from
a girl who knew the way to my heart. I
popped the cap off a bottle and drank
half of it. Jesus, the Dutch knew how to
live.*

—Robert B. Parker
God Save the Child

*May you always have a full belly,
a heavy purse, and a light heart.*

—traditional beer toast

78

The time when I feel most like a glass of beer is not in the evening when the pubs are open but at around four-thirty on a hot afternoon after wrestling with young cattle in some stifling cow-shed. It was delightful to retire, sweating and weary, to the shaded sanctuary of Mr. Worley's back kitchen and sip at the bitter ale, cool, frothing, straight from the cellar below.

—James Herriot
All Creatures Great and Small

The text of this book is set in Berkeley
with display in HotelModerne and
YvesScript,
by Mspace, Katonah, New York.

Book design by
Maura Fadden Rosenthal